Storytelling Guidance II

Five Reproducible Interactive Stories With Activities
For Young Children

WRITTEN BY
Melinda Villegas

ILLUSTRATED BY
Terry Sirrell

STORYTELLING GUIDANCE II

10-DIGIT ISBN: 1-57543-161-0   13-DIGIT ISBN: 978-1-57543-161-1

COPYRIGHT © 2008 MAR∗CO PRODUCTS, INC.
Published by mar∗co products, inc.
1443 Old York Road
Warminster, PA 18974
1-800-448-2197
www.marcoproducts.com

PERMISSION TO REPRODUCE: The purchaser may reproduce the activity sheets, free and without special permission, for participant use for a particular group or class. Reproduction of these materials for an entire school system is forbidden. All rights reserved. Except as provided above, no part of this book may be reproduced or transmitted in whole or in part in any form or by any means, electronic or mechanical, including photocopying, recording, or by any information storage or retrieval system without permission in writing by the publisher.

PRINTED IN THE U.S.A.

Contents

Storytelling Guidance II (Introduction)..4
    ASCA Standards For Storytelling Guidance II..5

Quinton's Bad Words Lesson.. 6-7
    Quinton's Bad Words (Reproducible Story)..8-14
    Gumball Words (Reproducible Activity Sheet)...15
    Control Your Words (Reproducible Poster)...16

The Rainbow Lesson... 17-19
    The Rainbow (Reproducible Story)...20-25
    Cooperation Poster (Reproducible Poster)..26
    Group Mural (Reproducible Activity Sheet)...27
    Compromising Situations (Reproducible Activity Sheet)..28

Kind Kurt Lesson... 29-30
    Kind Kurt (Reproducible Story)..31-39
    Friend Grab Cards (Reproducible Game Cards)..40-44
    Make A New Friend (Reproducible Poster).. 45

Terry's Old Clothes Lesson... 46-47
    Terry's Old Clothes (Reproducible Story)..48-54
    Friendship Puzzle (Reproducible Activity Sheet)..55

Use Your Kind Words Lesson... 56-58
    Use Your Kind Words (Reproducible Story)...59-66
    Use Your Kind Words (Reproducible Poster)...67
    Play Ball! (Reproducible Activity Sheet)..68-69
    What Would You Do? (Reproducible Activity Sheet)... 70
    Stop Unkind Words (Reproducible Activity Sheet)...71

About The Author... 72

Storytelling Guidance II
Introduction

The five stories included in *Storytelling Guidance II* emphasize behaviors which, if instilled at an early age, will enhance any child's educational experience.

Young children love having their own storybooks, and these stories are meant to be reproduced. Their format is designed to allow each child to grasp the meaning of each story as well as of the comprehension and self-insight questions and activities that punctuate the text. By completing the activities or questions and coloring the pictures, each child creates a personal book to read over and over again and share with his/her parents.

Conclude each lesson with the follow-up activities the stories include.

If you feel that reproducing the stories for the children in your classes is not appropriate, read the stories aloud to the children. In this case, you may first wish to reproduce the material, bind it, and color the pictures. When making a presentation of this kind, stop and elicit answers to the questions presented throughout the stories.

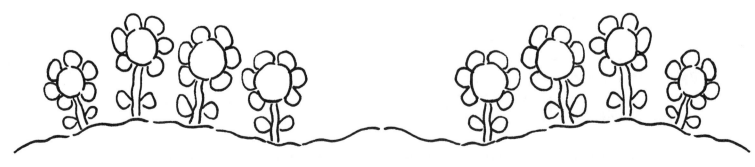

ASCA National Standards For Storytelling Guidance II

PERSONAL/SOCIAL DEVELOPMENT

		QUINTON'S BAD WORDS	THE RAINBOW	KIND KURT	TERRY'S OLD CLOTHES	USE YOUR KIND WORDS
Standard A: Students will acquire the knowledge, attitudes and interpersonal skills to help them understand and respect self and others.						
PS:A1	**Acquire Self-Knowledge**					
PS:A1.1	Develop positive attitudes toward self as a unique and worthy person	☒	☒	☒	☒	
PS:A1.2	Identify values, attitudes and beliefs	☒	☒	☒	☒	☒
PS:A1.3	Learn the goal-setting process	☒		☒	☒	
PS:A1.5	Identify and express feelings	☒		☒	☒	☒
PS:A1.6	Distinguish between appropriate and inappropriate behavior	☒	☒	☒	☒	☒
PS:A1.8	Understand the need for self-control and how to practice	☒		☒		
PS:A1.9	Demonstrate cooperative behavior in groups	☒	☒	☒		
PS:A1.10	Identify personal strengths and assets	☒	☒	☒	☒	
PS:A1.11	Identify and discuss changing personal and social roles	☒				
PS:A2	**Acquire Interpersonal Skills**					
PS:A2.1	Recognize that everyone has rights and responsibilities		☒	☒		
PS:A2.2	Respect alternative points of view		☒			
PS:A2.3	Recognize, accept, respect and appreciate individual differences				☒	
PS:A2.6	Use effective communications skills	☒	☒	☒		☒
PS:A2.8	Learn how to make and keep friends	☒	☒	☒	☒	☒
Standard B: Students will make decisions, set goals and take necessary action to achieve goals.						
PS:B1	**Self-Knowledge Application**					
PS:B1.1	Use a decision-making and problem-solving model	☒		☒		☒
PS:B1.2	Understand consequences of decisions and choices	☒		☒		☒
PS:B1.3	Identify alternative solutions to a problem	☒	☒			
PS:B1.4	Develop effective coping skills for dealing with problems	☒			☒	
PS:B1.7	Demonstrate a respect and appreciation for individual and cultural differences				☒	
PS:B1.8	Know when peer pressure is influencing a decision				☒	
PS:B1.9	Identify long- and short-term goals	☒				
PS:B1.10	Identify alternative ways of achieving goals	☒				
PS:B1.11	Use persistence and perseverance in acquiring knowledge and skills	☒				
PS:B1.12	Develop an action plan to set and achieve realistic goals	☒		☒	☒	
Standard C: Students will understand safety and survival skills.						
PS:C1	**Acquire Personal Safety Skills**					
PS:C1.7	Apply effective problem-solving and decision-making skills to make safe and healthy choices	☒	☒			☒
PS:C1.10	Learn techniques for managing stress and conflict	☒			☒	
PS:C1.11	Learn coping skills for managing life events	☒			☒	☒

Quinton's Bad Words

Objective:

Children will learn that:

- bad language is not acceptable
- using bad language offends others
- there are things they can do to control themselves when they feel like using bad language

Materials Needed:

For the leader:

None

For each student:

- Copy of *Quinton's Bad Words* (pages 8-14)
- Copy of *Gumball Words* (page 15)
- Copy of *Control Your Words* (page 16)
- Pencil
- Crayons
- Scissors
- Gluestick or paste

Presentation Preparation:

Reproduce *Quinton's Bad Words, Gumball Words,* and *Control Your Words* for each student. Make sure each student has a pencil and crayons. Gather the other necessary materials.

Lesson:

Ask the children the following questions, pausing to allow time for answers:

Do you ever get angry and use bad language?

Do you think that someone who uses bad language is pleasant to be around?

Then continue the lesson by saying:

Today we are going to read a story about a boy named Quinton. Quinton uses bad words, and he finds that he is losing friends because of his language. Quinton does not want this to happen. So, in our story, Quinton makes the important decision to stop using bad language. When we read the story, we will find out what Quinton did to make himself stop using bad words.

Give each student a copy of *Quinton's Bad Words*. Make sure each student has a pencil and crayons.

Read the story with the children, stopping to allow the children to complete the activity on each page.

Give each student a copy of *Gumball Words*, scissors, and paste. Instruct the students to cut out the gumballs that have nice words written on them and paste each one on the gumball machine. The children may then color the activity sheet.

Give each student a copy of *Control Your Words*. Review the information on the poster and tell the students to place the poster, at school or at home, where they can see it and be reminded not to use bad language.

Collect any materials distributed to the students and allow the students to take home their interactive story, poster, and activity sheet.

Quinton's Bad Words

Bad words aren't so bad
If you keep them inside.
But once they come out,
They have nowhere to hide.

They ring heavy in ears
That hear them all day.
And listeners may decide
To repeat them some way.

"I don't want to be your friend!"
And "Go away!"
Are a few bad words
That kids often say.

Then there are the really big ones
That are nasty and bad.
If you use those words,
You'll make everyone mad.

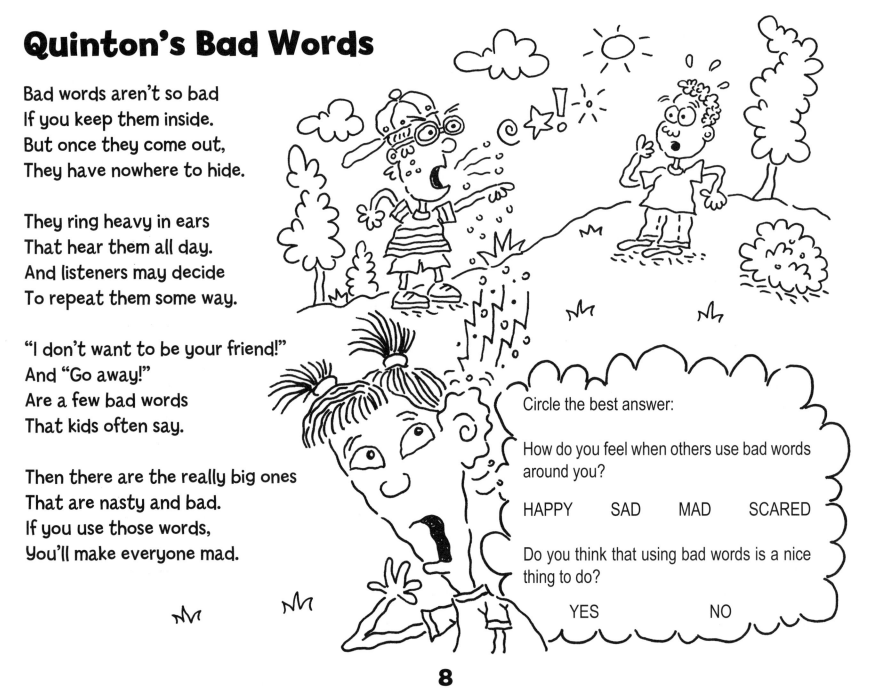

Circle the best answer:

How do you feel when others use bad words around you?

HAPPY   SAD   MAD   SCARED

Do you think that using bad words is a nice thing to do?

YES   NO

Quinton was a boy
Who chose to use words
That surprised everyone
When they were heard.

Bad words, nasty words
Spluttered out of his mouth
Every time he was angry,
Without any doubt.

But why was Quinton using those words?

The kids didn't like them.
They made his parents mad.
And every time Quinton used them,
They made him feel sad.

Draw an X on the face that shows how others felt when Quinton used bad words. Then circle the face that shows how Quinton felt when he used bad words.

"You'll find yourself all alone," said Mom,
"If bad words you choose to voice.
Cooling down when you are mad
Is a much, much better choice."

Quinton knew he had to try
Or he would not have one friend.
So he made up his mind
That the bad words would end.

Underline the sentence that tells what Quinton's mother said he needed to do.

1. Quinton's mother told him to cool down when he was angry.
2. Quinton's mother told him to keep using bad words.
3. Quinton's mother told him to fight when he was angry.

When Quinton became angry,
He would just walk away.
Or he would count to 10
If he had to stay.

No bad words came out
Of his mouth that day.
No ugly, nasty words
Not even one, did he say.

NO BAD WORDS WILL I SAY. NOT EVEN ONE THIS WHOLE DAY.

Circle the two things that Quinton did when he became angry.

"I'm quite proud of you, Quinton,"
Said Mom in words that were true.
"And I really am hoping with
Bad words you're through."

"Not to worry," said Quinton,
"Because I have a plan.
I'll write the words down
And throw them in a trash can.

"So if I ever have the urge
A bad word to say,
I'll write it down, rip it up,
And throw it away."

On the paper, write a behavior you have that you are not proud of. After you have written it down, make up your mind to never repeat it. Imagine throwing that behavior away.

That is exactly
What Quinton did do.
His parents are glad.
He has lots of friends, too.

Quinton figured out a way
To get rid of words that were bad.
He's made everyone happy.
And best of all, he's no longer sad.

Gumball Words

Directions: Read the words around the gumball machine. Cut out the nice words and paste them in the gumball machine.

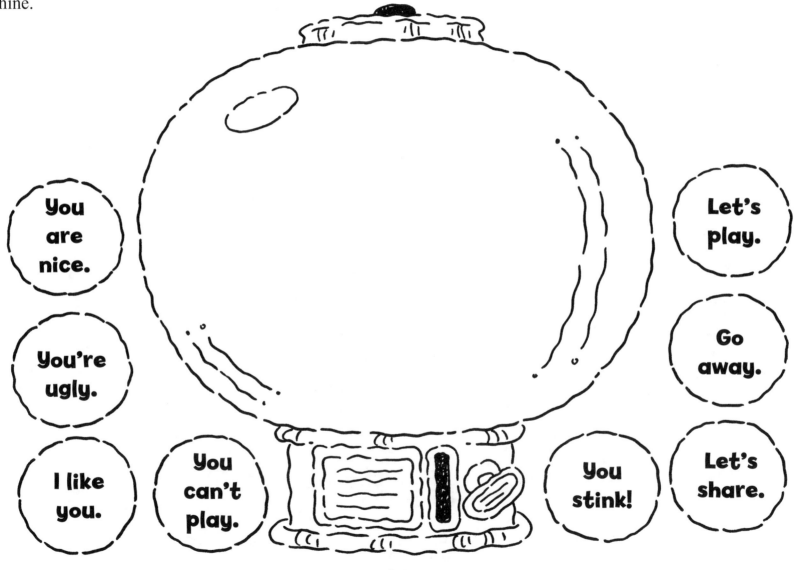

The Rainbow

Objective:

Children will learn:

- that they can accomplish a lot when they cooperate with one another during group work
- the importance of compromising with one another when they disagree

Materials Needed:

For the leader:

None

For each student:

- Copy of *The Rainbow* (pages 20-25)
- Copy of *Cooperation Poster* (page 26)
- Pencil
- Crayons that include red, orange, yellow, green, blue, indigo, and violet

For each student group:

- Copy of *Group Mural* (page 27)
- Copy of *Compromising Situations* (page 28)
- Piece of unlined paper
- Gluesticks or paste
- Scissors

17

Storytelling Guidance II © 2008 Mar∗co Products, Inc. 1.800.448.2197

Presentation Preparation:

Reproduce *The Rainbow* and *Cooperation Poster* for each student. Reproduce *Group Mural* and *Compromising Situations* for each group of students. Make sure each student has a pencil and crayons. Gather the other necessary materials.

Lesson:

Ask the children the following question, pausing to allow time for answers:

> *How many of you enjoy looking at rainbows?*

Then continue the lesson by saying:

> *A rainbow is wonderful to see. The colors blend together to form a beautiful, peaceful picture. Did you know children can be a lot like a rainbow? They can. When children work and play well together, they can appear just as beautiful and peaceful as a rainbow.*
>
> *Today we are going to read a story that will help us learn how to cooperate with one another so that we can work well in groups.*

Give each student a copy of *The Rainbow*. Make sure each child has a pencil and crayons.

Read the story with the children, stopping at the end of each page to allow the children to complete the activity.

Give each student a copy of the *Cooperation Poster*. Teach the students the rules for cooperation that are written on the rainbow.

Divide the students into groups of two to four members. Give each group a copy of *Group Mural*, a piece of unlined paper, scissors, and paste. Instruct the students to work together to create a group mural by coloring the pictures, cutting them out, and pasting them on the unlined paper. When the students have completed their murals, have some or all of the groups share their work with the class.

Divide the students into new groups of two to four members. Give each student group a copy of *Compromising Situations*. Tell the students to look at the two ways each person wants to resolve the situation, then work together to reach a compromise that will satisfy everyone. Have the students write their compromise in the rectangle below the descriptions of the two situations. Have some or all of the groups share their work with the class.

Instruct the students to take their story and activity sheets home. Each group must decide which student may keep the group's activity sheet. Collect any distributed materials.

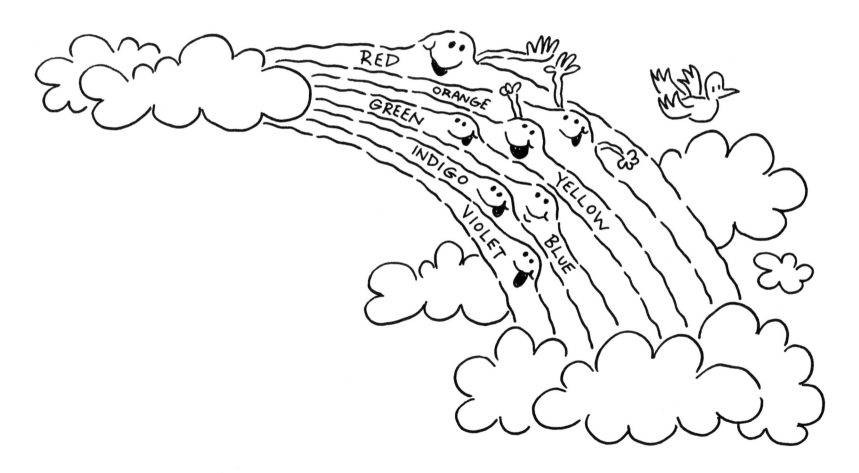

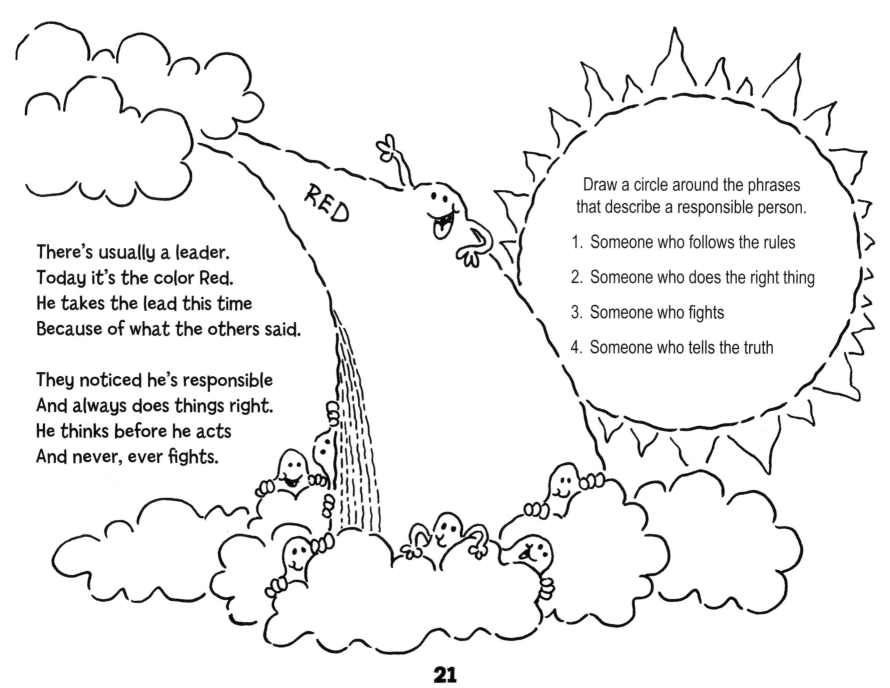

Unscramble the words below to see one way the colors helped each other.

___ _ __ __ ____
LAKT TI VREO

Color the first band of the rainbow the color that was the leader.

When it's time to form the rainbow,
Red issues his command.
The others all get ready
To lend a helping hand.

The leader's always first
So Red gets up and leaves the rest.
The others talk it over
To see who should join Red next.

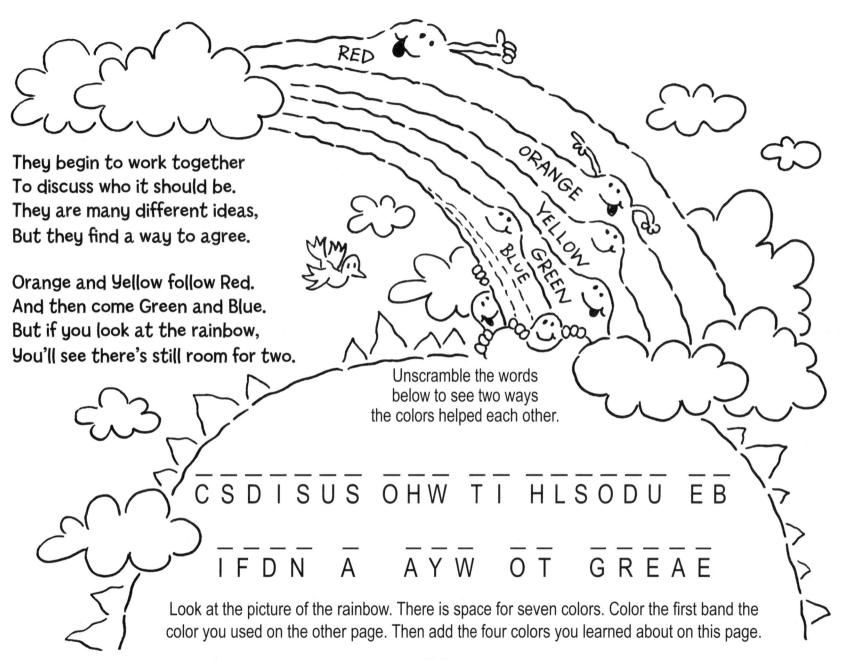

They begin to work together
To discuss who it should be.
They are many different ideas,
But they find a way to agree.

Orange and Yellow follow Red.
And then come Green and Blue.
But if you look at the rainbow,
You'll see there's still room for two.

Unscramble the words below to see two ways the colors helped each other.

_ _ _ _ _ _ _   _ _ _   _ _   _ _ _ _ _ _   _ _
C S D I S U S   O H W   T I   H L S O D U   E B

_ _ _ _   _   _ _ _   _ _   _ _ _ _ _
I F D N   A   A Y W   O T   G R E A E

Look at the picture of the rainbow. There is space for seven colors. Color the first band the color you used on the other page. Then add the four colors you learned about on this page.

23

Storytelling Guidance II © 2008 Mar✶co Products, Inc. 1.800.448.2197

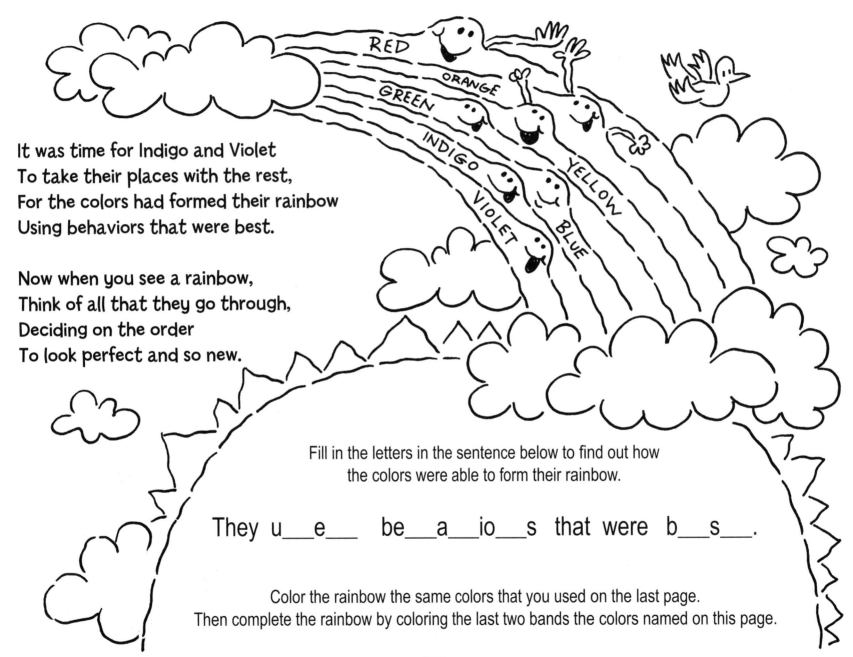

It was time for Indigo and Violet
To take their places with the rest,
For the colors had formed their rainbow
Using behaviors that were best.

Now when you see a rainbow,
Think of all that they go through,
Deciding on the order
To look perfect and so new.

Fill in the letters in the sentence below to find out how the colors were able to form their rainbow.

They u__e__ be__a__io__s that were b__s__.

Color the rainbow the same colors that you used on the last page.
Then complete the rainbow by coloring the last two bands the colors named on this page.

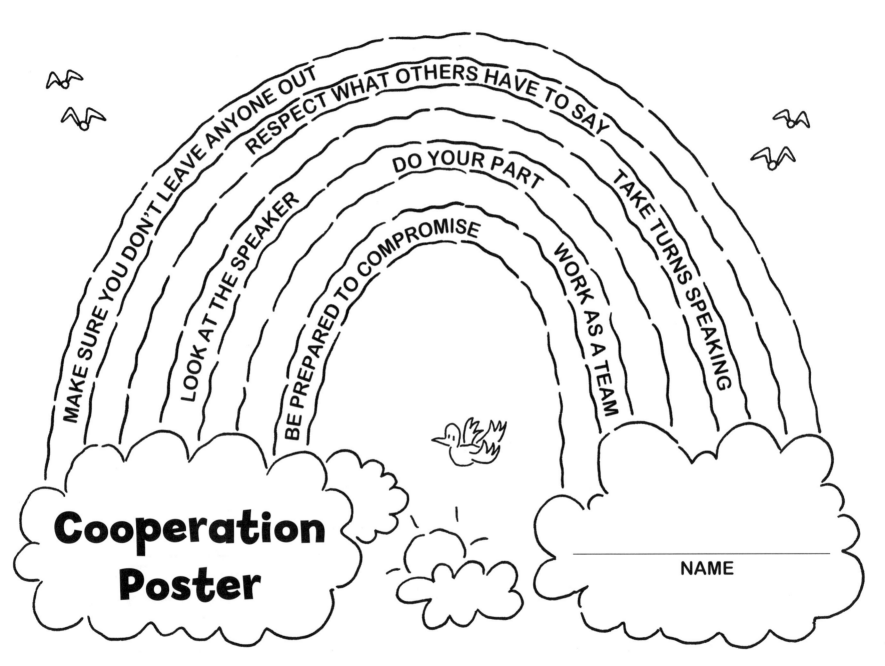

Group Mural

Compromising Situations

Names of Group Members:

_____   _____

_____   _____

Directions: Read both sides of each description below. As a group, work to decide on a compromise for each situation. Write your compromise in the box below the descriptions.

| You want to be the leader of the group. | Your friend wants to be leader of the group. |

| You would like to write the description of your project. | Your friend thinks your writing is too messy. |

| You want to turn in your project one day early. | Your friend wants to turn in the project on the day it is due. |

Kind Kurt

Objective:

Children will learn that:

- they can make friends by being kind to others
- they can decide to change and control the behaviors that prevent them from making and keeping friends

Materials Needed:

For the leader:

- *Friend Grab Cards* (pages 40-44)
- Bag
- Scissors

For each student:

- Copy of *Kind Kurt* (pages 31-39)
- Copy of *Make A New Friend* (page 45)
- Pencil
- Crayons

Presentation Preparation:

Reproduce the *Friend Grab Cards*. Cut apart the cards and place them in the bag. Reproduce *Kind Kurt* and *Make A New Friend* for each student. Make sure each student has a pencil and crayons.

Lesson:

Introduce the lesson by showing the students the bag of cards. Then say:

Each card in this bag describes a way to make or lose a friend. Each of you will draw a card, read it aloud, and tell if it describes a good way to make or lose a friend. (The leader may have to help with the reading.)

When you have completed the activity, continue the lesson by saying:

Each of you makes choices about your behavior. The choices you make will either help you make friends or cause you to lose friends. Remember: You make the choice; you are in control. Everything is up to you.

Today we are going to read a story about two boys. One of these boys has lots of friends. The other boy has none.

Give each student a copy of *Kind Kurt*. Make sure each child has a pencil and crayons.

Read the story with the children, stopping at the end of each page to allow the children to complete the activity.

Give each student a copy of the *Making New Friends* poster. Review the steps listed on the poster that will help the students make new friends.

Instruct the students to take their story and activity sheets home. Collect any distributed materials.

Kind Kurt

Kurt was as kind
As anyone could be.
He always said "Thank you"
And "May I have that, please?"

While Rudy was rude
And as ugly as could be.
He always said "Get away!"
And "Give that to me!"

Look at the pictures of Kind Kurt and Rude Rudy. Circle the one that shows whom you would pick for a friend.

When Kurt played with others
He made sure that he shared.
And if someone got hurt,
He showed that he really cared.

While Rudy would laugh
If somebody fell.
He'd pick on others
And hit them as well.

Write the words that fit on the blank lines.

In order to keep friends, you should __ h __ __ e

and c __ __ __.

To lose friends, you should __ __ __ k o __

them and __ i __ them.

Kurt had so many friends
Who would invite him to play,
That from morning 'till night
It was usually a great day.

Rudy got into fights
With others each day.
He was always in trouble
So he had no time to play.

Follow the path from your house to your friend's house. Remember not to step off the path.

"I don't like Kurt,"
Said Rudy one day.
"He has so many friends
Who invite him to play."

"I really like Rudy,"
Said Kurt one day.
"The next time I see him,
I'll ask him to play."

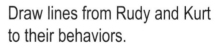

Draw lines from Rudy and Kurt to their behaviors.

When Rudy saw Kurt
He gave a fierce, mean look.
Rudy clenched his fist
And Kurt quivered and shook.

But when Kurt saw Rudy
He said "Hello."
"Let's play," he suggested
In a voice really low.

Circle your answer to the questions:

Would you ask a bully to play with you?
YES   NO

Do you think Rudy will play with Kurt?
YES   NO

Rudy was surprised
He'd been noticed that day.
So he quickly agreed
That he'd like to play.

He noticed that Kurt
Was so nice to him.
He let him go first
On the jungle gym.

Find the words hidden in the wordfind and circle them.
They will help you make friends.

BE NICE   SHARE   CARE   HELP   SMILE

```
B B N O I C A Z L Q
E R E N V F L E S F
N X C E U S S W M O
I T S H A R E X I T
C L E B E K L M L C
E D T T U C X R E L
X C A R E D A W L Y
T H E L P E B M K X
```

Rudy couldn't believe
How he felt that day.
He had his best day ever
And was heard to say

"I'm going to be
More like Kurt.
I'll treat others nicely
And help when they hurt."

Read the sentences below and decide if Rudy is being helpful or not. Circle "yes" if the thought is helpful. Circle "no" if the thought is not helpful.

I don't want to play with you!	YES	NO
Would you like to come to my party?	YES	NO
Do you need help with your math work?	YES	NO
Would you like some of my snack?	YES	NO

And so Rudy tried hard
To be nice all the time.
And smiling at others
Made him feel fine.

He practiced and practiced
To be nice each day.
And one day he noticed
It was his natural way.

Circle the pictures that show behaviors that help make friends.

So if making or keeping friends
Is hard for you,
Answer these questions
You'll know what to do.

What must I change?
Can I be nice and help out?
The answers are what
Friendship is all about.

Friend Grab Cards

You tell others they look nice. **Friend Grab Card—*Storytelling Guidance II*** © 2008 Mar∗co Products, Inc.	You calm down when you are angry. **Friend Grab Card—*Storytelling Guidance II*** © 2008 Mar∗co Products, Inc.
You smile at others. **Friend Grab Card—*Storytelling Guidance II*** © 2008 Mar∗co Products, Inc.	You frown at others. **Friend Grab Card—*Storytelling Guidance II*** © 2008 Mar∗co Products, Inc.
You always use nice words. **Friend Grab Card—*Storytelling Guidance II*** © 2008 Mar∗co Products, Inc.	You stomp your feet when you are angry. **Friend Grab Card—*Storytelling Guidance II*** © 2008 Mar∗co Products, Inc.

Friend Grab Cards

You yawn when others speak. **Friend Grab Card—*Storytelling Guidance II*** © 2008 Mar*co Products, Inc.	You give compliments to others. **Friend Grab Card—*Storytelling Guidance II*** © 2008 Mar*co Products, Inc.
You scream at others when you are angry. **Friend Grab Card—*Storytelling Guidance II*** © 2008 Mar*co Products, Inc.	You let everyone play. **Friend Grab Card—*Storytelling Guidance II*** © 2008 Mar*co Products, Inc.
You thank others when they give you something. **Friend Grab Card—*Storytelling Guidance II*** © 2008 Mar*co Products, Inc.	You tell others to leave you alone. **Friend Grab Card—*Storytelling Guidance II*** © 2008 Mar*co Products, Inc.

Friend Grab Cards

You tell others to go away. **Friend Grab Card—***Storytelling Guidance II* © 2008 Mar∗co Products, Inc.	You help others when they need help. **Friend Grab Card—***Storytelling Guidance II* © 2008 Mar∗co Products, Inc.
You hit others when you are angry. **Friend Grab Card—***Storytelling Guidance II* © 2008 Mar∗co Products, Inc.	You invite your whole class to your birthday party. **Friend Grab Card—***Storytelling Guidance II* © 2008 Mar∗co Products, Inc.
You share with others. **Friend Grab Card—***Storytelling Guidance II* © 2008 Mar∗co Products, Inc.	You tease others. **Friend Grab Card—***Storytelling Guidance II* © 2008 Mar∗co Products, Inc.

Friend Grab Cards

You talk with a new student. **Friend Grab Card—***Storytelling Guidance II* © 2008 Mar∗co Products, Inc.	You help others when they fall. **Friend Grab Card—***Storytelling Guidance II* © 2008 Mar∗co Products, Inc.
You tell others their clothes are ugly when you don't like what they're wearing. **Friend Grab Card—***Storytelling Guidance II* © 2008 Mar∗co Products, Inc.	You cheer up someone who is sad. **Friend Grab Card—***Storytelling Guidance II* © 2008 Mar∗co Products, Inc.
You trip others to see them fall. **Friend Grab Card—***Storytelling Guidance II* © 2008 Mar∗co Products, Inc.	You laugh at others when they cry. **Friend Grab Card—***Storytelling Guidance II* © 2008 Mar∗co Products, Inc.

Friend Grab Cards

You don't share when you have a snack and others don't. *Friend Grab Card—Storytelling Guidance II* © 2008 Mar*co Products, Inc.	You tattle on your friends. *Friend Grab Card—Storytelling Guidance II* © 2008 Mar*co Products, Inc.
You share when others don't have a snack. *Friend Grab Card—Storytelling Guidance II* © 2008 Mar*co Products, Inc.	You talk with others when they are sad. *Friend Grab Card—Storytelling Guidance II* © 2008 Mar*co Products, Inc.
You say you are sorry when you have done something wrong. *Friend Grab Card—Storytelling Guidance II* © 2008 Mar*co Products, Inc.	You never leave anyone out. *Friend Grab Card—Storytelling Guidance II* © 2008 Mar*co Products, Inc.

Terry's Old Clothes

Objective:

Children will learn to:

- accept the differences in others
- judge others by their character, not their outward appearance

Materials Needed:

For the leader:

- Shiny red apple

For each student:

- Copy of *Terry's Old Clothes* (pages 48-54)
- Copy *of Friendship Puzzle* (page 55)
- Pencil
- Crayons
- Scissors
- Envelope

Presentation Preparation:

Reproduce *Terry's Old Clothes* and the *Friendship Puzzle* for each student. Make sure each student has a pencil and crayons. Gather the other necessary materials.

Lesson:

Show the students your apple. Then ask:

Who can tell me how this apple looks? (The apple looks shiny, nice, and any other appropriate answers.)

Do you think the apple is just as nice on the inside? (No one can tell until the apple is sliced open.)

Continue the lesson by saying:

That is correct. Sometimes an apple is just as nice on the inside as it is on the outside. But sometimes an apple is rotten and tastes awful. You really can't judge how the apple will taste by the way it looks on the outside.

People are like that, too. Someone who has a beautiful face might be really mean and rude to others. Just because someone is beautiful on the outside doesn't mean he or she is beautiful on the inside.

What do you think is more important: being beautiful on the inside or on the outside? (Being beautiful on the inside by being kind and friendly to others is more important because it will help you make and keep friends.)

Today we are going to read a story about a girl named Terry. People judge Terry by the clothes she wears. Even though Terry feels awful, she still finds a way to make friends. Let's read the story to find out what Terry does.

Give each student a copy of *Terry's Old Clothes*. Make sure each student has a pencil and crayons.

Read the story with the children, stopping at the end of each page to allow time for the children to complete the activity.

Give each student a copy of the *Friendship Puzzle*, scissors, and an envelope. Have the students color the picture, then cut it apart. Have the students mix up their pieces then put the puzzle together again. When the students have completed their puzzles, have them put the pieces into the envelope. If this activity is not challenging enough for your group, tell the students to cut their puzzles along the lines given, then cut each piece in half. This will make eight pieces. You may then have the students put the puzzle together themselves or exchange their puzzle pieces with a classmate.

Instruct the students to take their story and activity sheets home. Collect any distributed materials.

Terry's Old Clothes

Terry wore old clothes,
But they were always very clean.
Her sneakers had two holes,
And they were the color green.

She wore the sneakers every day.
They were the only shoes she had.
But if you looked upon her face,
She was never really sad.

Circle the picture that shows how Terry feels.

Her smile was big and friendly
And everything seemed OK
Until she went to school
And heard what others had to say.

"Your clothes are old and ugly.
Get away, you cannot play.
This game is for girls with pretty clothes,"
Is what they had to say.

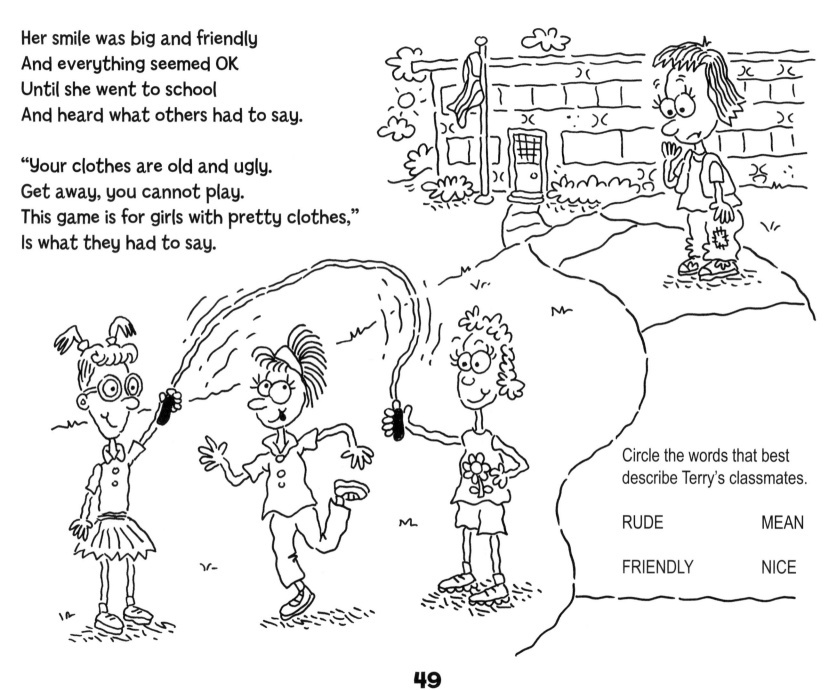

Circle the words that best describe Terry's classmates.

RUDE   MEAN

FRIENDLY   NICE

In class, it was no different.
When the teacher was not around.
The girls would laugh and snicker,
Look at Terry and make a frown.

Sure, the words hurt Terry.
They hurt her very much.
But Terry made a choice that day
And she kept her feelings hushed.

"I'll smile at everyone," she thought,
"And share the little I've got.
I'll talk with each girl one by one,
And show I care a lot."

Circle the picture that shows Terry's plan.

And so when Karen fell,
Terry helped her off the floor.
She gave Janice extra paper
When she needed more.

She listened to the teacher
And she completed all her work.
And when she finished early,
She helped others without a smirk.

Look at each of the pictures. Each picture stands for a letter. Write the letter on the blank above the picture. Then you will know Terry's plan.

- 📄 = r
- ✏️ = d
- 📏 = o
- ✂️ = b
- 🖍️ = i

Te__ __ y __ e c i __ e __

t__ __ e n__c e.

It didn't take others long
To see Terry's bright smile.
And her warm and caring ways
Were noticed after a while.

"I really do like Terry,"
Thought Mary Lou one day.
"I think that right after lunch,
I'll ask her to play."

The others started noticing
That Terry had a friend.
And it wasn't very long
Before their rules began to bend.

Look at the hopscotch game. Color the squares that show games or activities in which the children might include Terry.

Terry's clothes now didn't matter.
The girls no longer stared.
Instead they all began to show
They really, truly cared.

They began to like Terry
For her very great big heart
That sadly they failed
To notice from the very start.

Follow the letters of the alphabet, beginning with "A," to see what made the others like Terry.

So if you're feeling bad
Because others have more than you,
Don't spend your time being unhappy,
Discouraged, or feeling blue.

Use what you've got inside
To be the best that people see.
Others will notice and come around
And friends to you they'll be.

Fill the heart with nice things you can do for others.

Friendship Puzzle

Directions: Color the picture, then cut it out along the dark lines. Now you have a puzzle. Have fun putting the puzzle together. When you are finished, put your puzzle pieces into the envelope so you can put it together again at home.

Use Your Kind Words

Objective:

Children will learn that:

- using kind words is a great way to resolve any kind of conflict
- using kind words can prevent friendship problems

Materials Needed:

For the leader:

None

For each student:

- Copy of *Use Your Kind Words* (pages 59-66)
- Copy of *Use Your Kind Words Poster* (page 67)
- Copy of *Play Ball!* (optional, pages 68-69)
- Copy of *What Would You Do?* (optional, page 70)
- Copy of *Stop Unkind Words* (optional, pages 71)
- Pencil
- Crayons
- Scissors (optional)
- Gluestick or paste (optional)

Presentation Preparation:

Reproduce *Use Your Kind Words* and the *Use Your Kind Words Poster* for each student. If you are presenting any of the optional activities, reproduce *Play Ball!*, *What Would You Do?*, and/or *Stop Unkind Words* for each student. Make sure each student has a pencil and crayons. Gather the other necessary materials.

Lesson:

Introduce the lesson by asking the students:

> ***Who can tell me what the word* conflict *means?*** (A *conflict* can occur when two or more people or countries do not agree on something.)
>
> ***How many of you have had conflicts with your friends?***

Ask for a few students to volunteer to tell about a conflict they have had with friends. Tell them not to mention any names.

Continue the lesson by saying:

> ***Conflicts are as much a part of life as eating and sleeping. No one gets along with everyone all the time. If you do not know how to handle conflicts correctly, friendships can be lost or damaged. That is why today's lesson is so important. We are going to read a story that will help you know what to say when you find yourself in a conflict with a friend. Listen closely for ideas on how using nice words can help you handle your own conflicts successfully.***

Give each student a copy of *Use Your Kind Words*. Make sure each student has a pencil and crayons. Read the story with the children, stopping at the end of each page to allow the children to complete the activity.

Give each student a copy of the *Use Your Kind Words Poster*. Review the steps for resolving conflicts. Instruct the students to keep the poster in a place where they can look at it if they need to be reminded what to do when a conflict arises.

If time allows, present one or more of the following activities.

Give each student a copy of *Play Ball!*, scissors, and paste. Have the students cut out the baseballs that display kind words and glue them on the bat.

Give each student a copy of *What Would You Do?* Have the students read the descriptions and choose the best way to resolve each situation. When the students have completed the activity sheet, have them share their answers and give reasons for their choices.

Give each student a copy of *Stop Unkind Words*. Tell the students to read each statement, then color the traffic light to indicate whether the statement is unkind (red) or a kind (green).

Instruct the students to take their story and activity sheets home. Collect any distributed materials.

Use Your Kind Words

Using your kind words
Is a very, very smart way
To show others you control
Your actions each and every day.

You can use your kind words
In many different situations.
It just takes a little practice
And, of course, a little patience.

So instead of yelling, hitting, or arguing
When things don't go your way,
Remember to use kind words
And your friends will all stay.

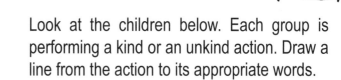

Look at the children below. Each group is performing a kind or an unkind action. Draw a line from the action to its appropriate words.

Want some cookies?

I don't like you!

Let's play!

Get out of here!

Playing ball
Is a lot of fun
Until someone grabs the ball,
Then decides to run.

Your first reaction
Might be to yell
Or to run to find
An adult to tell.

Complete the sentence by filling in the missing letters.

A child who takes a ball from someone else is called a
B___ ___ ___ Y.

Stop! Losing control
Is really not wise.
Instead, use your kind words
With these gals or guys.

"Playing ball with you
Is really great!"
Or "Let's play together!"
Is something you could state.

The kid might welcome
A friend with whom to play ball
Because kids who take balls from others
Have no friends at all.

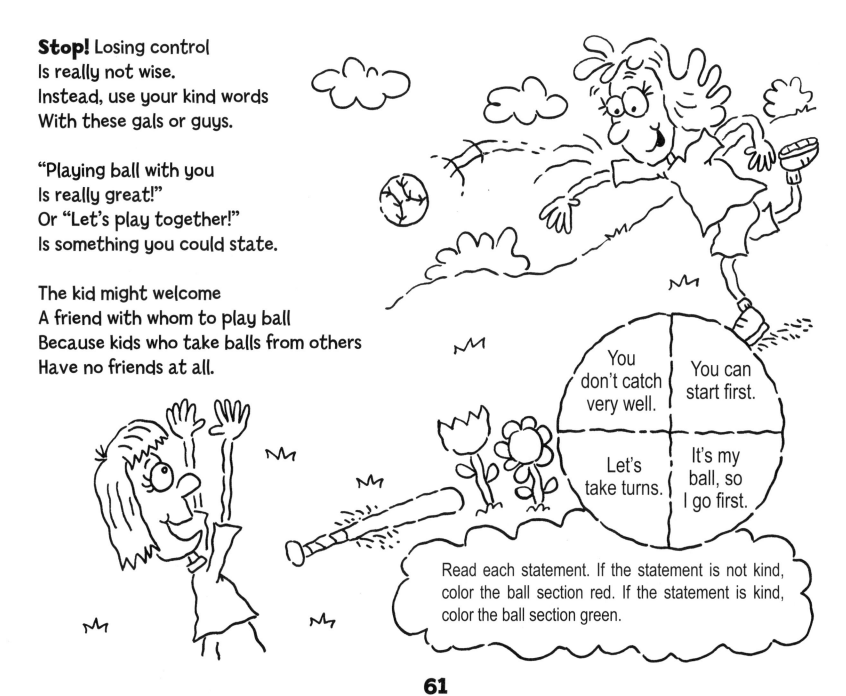

Read each statement. If the statement is not kind, color the ball section red. If the statement is kind, color the ball section green.

Lee loves to talk in class
But always at the wrong time.
When kids are reading or writing
Or walking down the hall in line.

If you feel like screaming,
Kicking, pushing, or hitting,
In the principal's office
You're soon be sitting.

Read the statements below. Underline those that follow classroom rules.

Raise your hand for permission to speak.

Speak in a loud voice.

Speak with your neighbor while the teacher is talking.

Use an indoor voice in the classroom.

Stop! Losing control
Is really not wise.
Instead, use your kind words
With these gals or guys.

"Your stories are great,"
Is what you might say.
"But tell me about them
When we go out to play."

Listening to others
At the right time
May help them keep
Quiet in class and in line.

On the picture, circle two body parts that help you to listen.

Being made fun of
Is not very cool
Especially when it happens
In front of others at school.

You might feel like crying,
Call names, or even curse.
But to do any of these
Will make the situation worse.

Circle the sentences that tell why crying, name-calling, or cursing would make the situation worse.

Kids might think you're a baby.

You might get into trouble.

It might start a fight.

It wouldn't stop the person from making fun of you.

Stop! Losing control
Is really not wise.
Walk away, ignore,
Or give these kind words a try...

"I'd like you to stop,
Bullying me this way.
Instead of calling me names,
Why don't we just play?"

Connect the dots with your pencil.

Stop bullying me.

Using kind words
May seem kind of hard.
But it really is not
If you stay on your guard.

Know that even though
Things can always go wrong,
To decide what to do
Doesn't have to take long.

Remember. Using kind words
Is the only sure way
To solve all your problems
And get on with your day.

Draw a line from each question to its best answer.

What should you do when you are angry?   Suggest that you share the ball.

What should you do when someone calls you a bad name?   Tell him/her to stop.

What should you do if someone takes something from you?   Calm down before speaking.

Use Your Kind Words

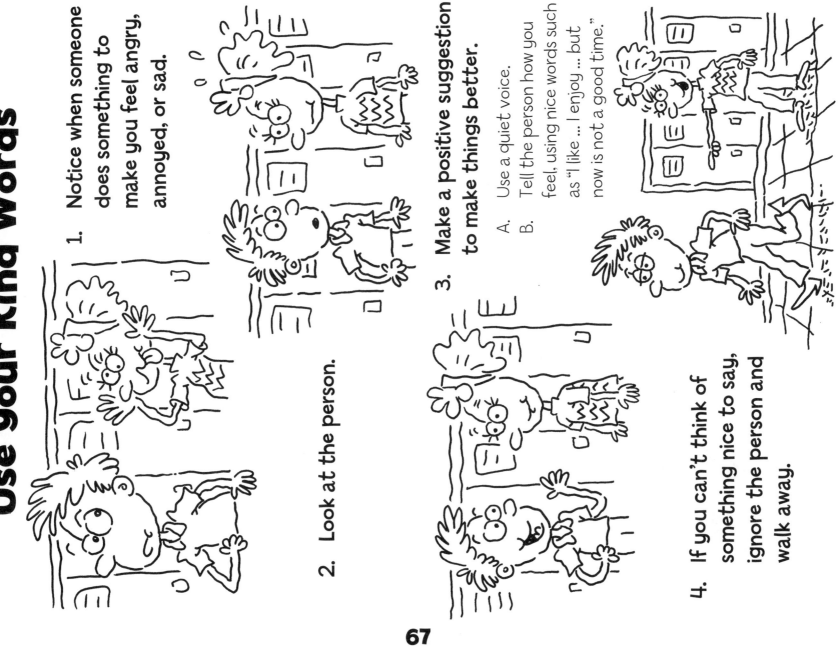

1. Notice when someone does something to make you feel angry, annoyed, or sad.

2. Look at the person.

3. Make a positive suggestion to make things better.

    A. Use a quiet voice.
    B. Tell the person how you feel, using nice words such as "I like ... I enjoy ... but now is not a good time."

4. If you can't think of something nice to say, ignore the person and walk away.

Play Ball!

Directions:

Read the statement on each baseball.
If the statement uses kind words,
cut it out and glue it to the bat.

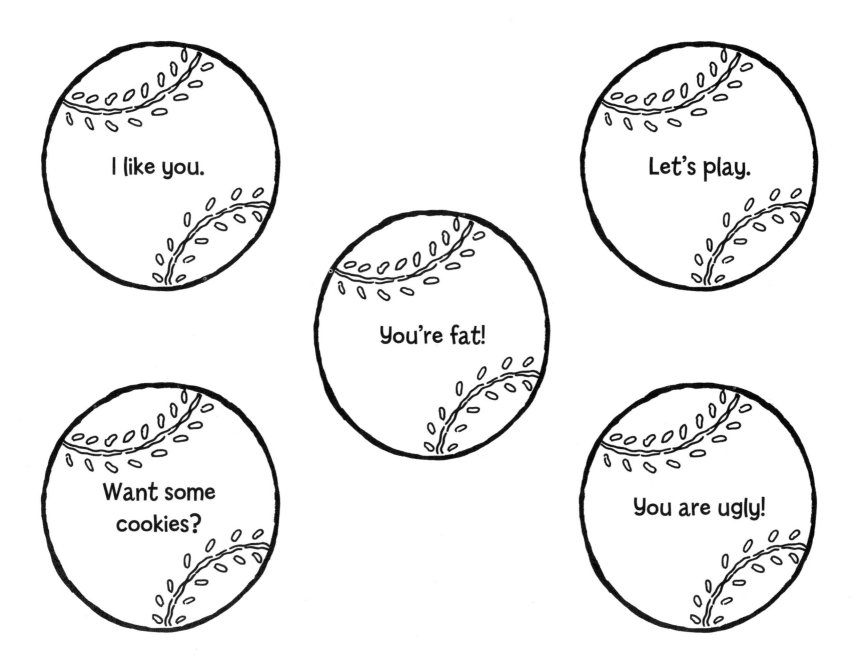

What Would You Do?

Directions: Read the description of each situation and the choices for solving the problem. Circle the answer you believe is best.

1. **Marty is teasing Melissa. How should Melissa handle the teasing?**

    a. Scream at Marty, "Leave me alone!"

    b. Stand there and cry.

    c. Look Marty in the eye and say "Marty, I don't like it when you make fun of me. I want you to stop."

2. **Carol wants the ball Mark is playing with. How should Mark handle this problem?**

    a. Run away.

    b. Look at Carol and ask, "Why don't we share the ball?"

    c. Kick Carol.

3. **Robbie suddenly grabs the book Monica is reading. How should Monica handle this problem?**

    a. Run after Robbie and take the book back.

    b. Run after Robbie and try to trip him.

    c. Tell Robbie, "I don't appreciate you taking my book without asking for it. Let's look at it together."

4. **Norma overhears a group of children laughing at her friend Laura. How should Norma handle this problem?**

    a. Look at the group of children and tell them it is not nice to talk about others.

    b. Run and tell Laura what the children are saying.

    c. Tell an adult what she heard.

5. **Terry makes a comment to Liz about her clothes being old. How should Liz handle this problem?**

    a. Look at Terry and say, "Your clothes are ugly, too."

    b. Cry.

    c. Ignore Terry.

Stop Unkind Words

Directions: Read each statement. Color the word *STOP* on the traffic light red if the words are unkind. Color the word *GO* on the traffic light green if the words are kind.

Melinda Villegas

The power and magic of storytelling have always intrigued me. Reading and listening to stories as a child opened up a whole new world for me. The characters were always so vivid, they seemed real. As I read different stories, I carried a part of the characters with me and still think of them today.

I can hear my mother's voice as she read the Golden Books to me over and over again. I found myself full of empathy, joyous, or intrigued because of something new each reading taught me.

As an educator, I use storytelling to teach my students skills that will help them become better individuals. And I hope that what I teach through storytelling will have a lasting impact on their lives.

Melinda Villegas is the author of *Storytelling Guidance* and *Powerful Puppetry,* both published by Mar*co Products. She is an elementary counselor in the McAllen Independent School District in Texas.